Dear Parents and Educators,

Welcome to Penguin Young Readers! As parents and educators, you know that each child develops at their own pace—in terms of speech, critical thinking, and, of course, reading. Penguin Young Readers recognizes this fact. As a result, each Penguin Young Readers book is assigned a traditional easy-to-read level (1–4) as well as an F&P Text Level (A–R). Both of these systems will help you choose the right book for your child. Please refer to the back of each book for specific leveling information. Penguin Young Readers features esteemed authors and illustrators, stories about favorite characters, fascinating nonfiction, and more!

Octopus! Smartest in the Sea?	LEVEL **4**
	F&P TEXT LEVEL **R**

This book is perfect for a **Fluent Reader** who:
- can read the text quickly with minimal effort;
- has good comprehension skills;
- can self-correct (can recognize when something doesn't sound right); and
- can read aloud smoothly and with expression.

Here are some **activities** you can do during and after reading this book:
- Creative Writing: Pretend you are giving a presentation to your class on the following topic: Do you think octopuses are the smartest creatures in the sea? Write a paragraph explaining why you think they are or why you think they are not.
- Nonfiction: Nonfiction books deal with facts and events that are real. Talk about the elements of nonfiction. Then, on a separate sheet of paper, write down the facts you learned about octopuses while reading.

Remember, sharing the love of reading with a child is the best gift you can give!

*This book has been officially leveled by using the F&P Text Level Gradient™ leveling system.

For author Sy Montgomery, whose scientific curiosity and creative writing have inspired me—GLC

PENGUIN YOUNG READERS
An imprint of Penguin Random House LLC, New York

First published in the United States of America by Penguin Young Readers,
an imprint of Penguin Random House LLC, New York, 2024

Text copyright © 2024 by Ginjer L. Clarke
Octopus arm illustrations by Kimberley Sampson, copyright © 2024 by Penguin Random House LLC

Photo credits: cover, 3: Subaqueosshutterbug/iStock/Getty Images; 4: (inset) Kevin Schafer/The Image Bank/Getty Images; 4–5: (background) MARK GARLICK/SCIENCE PHOTO LIBRARY/ Getty Images; 6–7: Jman78/iStock/Getty Images; 8: Paul Taylor/Stone/Getty Images; 10: Michele Westmorland/Corbis Documentary/Getty Images; 11: Ian_Redding/iStock/Getty Images; 12–13: Mark Newman/Lonely Planet RF/Getty Images; 14–15: Andrey Nekrasov/imageBROKER/ Getty Images; 17: Michael Zeigler/iStock/Getty Images; 18: Brandon Cole Marine Photography/ Alamy Stock Photo; 19: The Asahi Shimbun/Getty Images; 20: Daniel Lamborn/Alamy Stock Photo; 21: AndamanSE/iStock/Getty Images; 22: NOAA/Alamy Stock Photo; 23: atese/iStock/Getty Images; 24: Dave Collins/iStock/Getty Images; 25: Mark Conlin/Alamy Stock Photo; 27: Doug Perrine/Alamy Stock Photo; 28–29: Velvetfish/iStock/Getty Images; 30–31: AlexeyMasliy/iStock/Getty Images; 32–33, 34–35: ANESTIS REKKAS/Alamy Stock Photo; 36–37: Chris Gug/Alamy Stock Photo; 38: mikhail rudenko/ iStock/Getty Images; 39: Stuart Westmorland/Corbis Documentary/Getty Images; 40–41: JORGEN JESSEN/AFP/Getty Images; 42: Hal Beral/Corbis/Getty Images; 43: Reinhard Dirscherl/ullstein bild/ Getty Images; 44–45: Issaurinko/iStock/Getty Images; 46: tane-mahuta/iStock/Getty Images; 47: A. Martin UW Photography/Moment/Getty Images; 48: Douglas Klug/Moment Open/Getty Images

Visit us online at penguinrandomhouse.com.

Library of Congress Cataloging-in-Publication Data is available.

Manufactured in China

ISBN 9780593521977 (pbk)   10 9 8 7 6 5 4 3 2 1 WKT
ISBN 9780593521984 (hc)   10 9 8 7 6 5 4 3 2 1 WKT

OCTOPUS!

SMARTEST IN THE SEA?

by Ginjer L. Clarke

Octopuses are *very* old. They have been around for more than 350 million years—even before dinosaurs! Back then, they looked a little different. They had shells to protect their soft bodies. We know because people have found fossils, or prints in stone, of these shells.

Their shells slowly got thinner over time and disappeared about 65 million years ago, just after the time of dinosaurs. Octopuses got stronger and learned to hide. They also grew bigger brains.

Recently we have learned a lot more about these amazing, smart creatures. Let's find out what makes octopuses so special!

Ammonite fossils

Just Keep Swimming

Octopuses live in all of the world's oceans. Some swim in cold, deep water. Others crawl around warm, shallow seas. There are more than 300 types of octopuses. Some are huge and others are tiny. Octopuses belong to the family of cephalopods (say: SEF-ah-low-podz). This word means "head foot" because they seem to have legs attached to their heads, with no bodies. The word *octopus* means "eight feet."

An octopus really has eight arms, not feet. All of its arms are the same length. The arms can work together, or they can do different things at the same time. The octopus can even grow a new arm if one gets bitten off by a shark or a big fish.

Each arm is covered in two rows of suckers. The octopus grips, tastes, and feels with its thousands of strong suckers.

The top of the octopus is called its mantle. The mantle is a head and body all in one. Inside the mantle are three hearts. *Thump, thump!* They pump blue blood!

Something else is hiding inside the octopus's mantle—a beak! This sharp beak can bite through shells. *Chomp!* The beak is the only hard part of an octopus's body, as an octopus has no bones! An octopus also does not have ears, so it is deaf. But it can feel sounds in its body.

Another surprising part of the octopus is its eyes. Octopus eyes have sideways, rectangular pupils.

This shape helps the octopus see all around its body. It sees details very well, but it does not see like humans do. All octopuses are color-blind!

Octopuses cannot *see* colors, but they come in lots of colors. The giant Pacific octopus is bright red-orange. It is the largest of all octopuses. This big beauty can weigh hundreds of pounds. It can be up to 30 feet wide, from the tip of one arm to the tip of another when stretched out.

That is as long as a school bus!

Pop! This giant octopus opens a clamshell with its strong suckers. It can lift up to 30 pounds with just *one* of its sticky suckers.

It tastes everything it touches with its suckers. The suckers can taste 1,000 times better than a human tongue can.

The giant Pacific octopus crawls around a lot, touching things with its arms. But it is also a good swimmer. First the octopus pulls water into its mantle. *Push!* Then it blows water backward out of a tube behind its eye. The tube is called a siphon (say: SYE-fun).

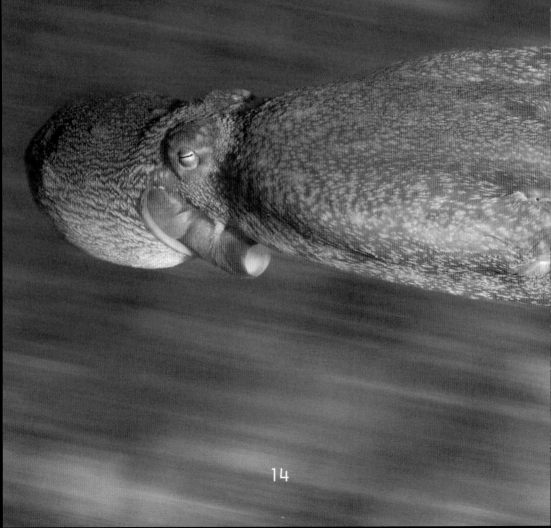

Whoosh! The octopus tucks in its arms and swims fast. This motion is called jet propulsion (say: pruh-PUL-shun). All octopuses swim in this way. Some planes, boats, and rockets move this way as well.

Growing Up or Staying Small

The giant Pacific octopus is the biggest octopus, but it starts life very small. One night, a female giant Pacific octopus lays about 50,000 eggs. She connects the eggs in long strings. She then sticks the eggs to the ceiling and sides of her den. Each tiny egg is only the size of a single grain of rice!

The mother octopus can spend almost a year caring for her eggs. *Fluff!* She cleans the eggs with the tips of her arms. *Puff!* She blows water on her eggs. She does not eat at all while she stays in the den to protect her eggs. So she dies once the baby octopuses all hatch.

Finally, the giant Pacific octopus babies break free from their eggs. They look like tiny copies of their mother. *Zoom!* They hide quickly to keep from being eaten by crabs and sea stars.

The mother octopus laid thousands of eggs, but most of the babies do get eaten. Only a few babies survive, and they can live to be up to five years old.

An adult giant Pacific octopus is almost fully grown in about one year. It can go from weighing less than a raindrop to more than 100 pounds. That makes it one of the fastest-growing animals on Earth!

Star-sucker
pygmy octopus

20

Some octopuses start small but never get much bigger. The world's smallest octopus is the star-sucker pygmy octopus. This little cutie is less than one inch long. It weighs less than a jelly bean!

The greater blue-ringed octopus is also tiny—about the size of a golf ball. But it is deadly! It bites when it feels threatened. It has venom that can kill both animals and people. Watch out! Its bright blue rings are a warning to keep away.

Dumbo octopuses have a funny name. They are named after the story of Dumbo, the flying elephant with big ears. Like Dumbo, these small octopuses have large, ear-like fins on their mantles. *Flap, flap!* The fins help these rare octopuses to fly through the very deep water where they live.

The wunderpus octopus is also small and extraordinary. Its name comes from the fact that it is a wonder of the octopus world. Every wunderpus has different stripes and spots. No two are alike. Cool!

Hiding from Danger

Even big octopuses have to be good at hide-and-seek. Many ocean creatures like to eat octopuses. Sharks, big fish, seals, moray eels, and humans are their main predators.

Here comes a giant moray eel. *Hurry!*

An octopus dives into its den on the seafloor. *Scurry!* It pushes some rocks in front of the opening to keep the eel from getting in.

Many octopuses make dens in mud, rocks, or the coral reef. Smaller octopuses sometimes live in empty shells or bottles. Giant Pacific octopuses often move into old shipwrecks.

Two-spot octopus

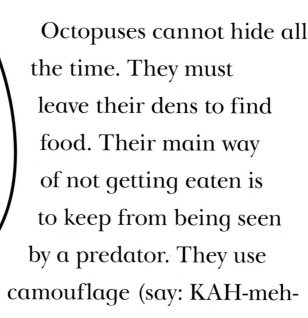

Octopuses cannot hide all the time. They must leave their dens to find food. Their main way of not getting eaten is to keep from being seen by a predator. They use camouflage (say: KAH-meh-flazh) to blend into whatever is around them.

A long-arm octopus matches its skin to the seafloor. *Flash!* This octopus changes color in less than a second. It makes stripes, spots, and patterns that move. It can change its look hundreds of times in an hour! This ability helps confuse its enemies.

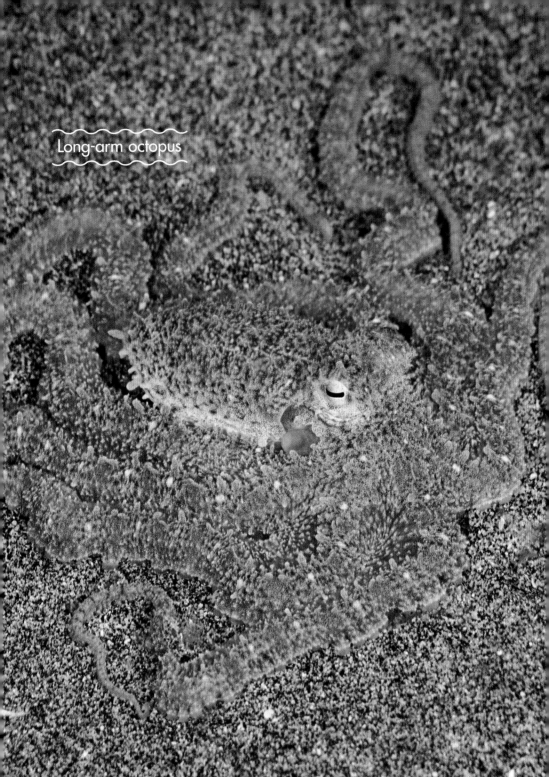

Long-arm octopus

Some octopuses also change shape to fool predators. They stretch out the skin between their arms to look much bigger.

A long-arm octopus pretends to be a starfish. *Twirl!* Young octopuses often twist their arms into coils to look like seaweed.

To *mimic* means to be like something else. Most animals can only mimic one other animal. The mimic octopus changes to look like many dangerous sea creatures. *Swirl!* It waves its arms to look like sea snakes. It can also mimic a flatfish, lionfish, or jellyfish.

Mimic octopus

Sometimes hiding does not work. A shark has spotted a giant Pacific octopus. The octopus jets away, but the shark keeps coming. The octopus squirts a cloud of thick black ink out of its siphon. *Poof!* It disappears into the darkness.

The ink blob confuses the shark, blocks its sense of smell, and irritates its eyes. The octopus escapes and swims away. It quickly camouflages in a new hiding place. *Phew!* That was a close one!

Common octopus

Hunting for Food

Octopuses get hunted, but they are also good hunters. Octopuses eat many creatures, including clams, squid, fish, birds, and other octopuses. Their favorite food is crabs.

An octopus watches from behind a rock. A crab scurries by. The octopus spreads out its arms like an umbrella. *Boom!* It lands on the crab and grabs it.

The octopus crawls back to its den with the crab. *Crack!* It breaks the crab's shell with its beak. It squirts poisonous spit inside the crab. Then its sucks out the crab's guts!

Some animals the octopus eats have harder shells. This means the octopus needs another trick to get a tasty treat. It has a row of teeth on its tongue called a radula (say: RAD-joo-luh). The radula is like an octopus drill.

Whir! The octopus makes a tiny hole in a clamshell with its radula. This process can take an hour! Then the octopus injects its venom to loosen the clam. The octopus opens the shell and sucks out the clam. *Slurp!* Finally, it places the shell onto a pile outside its den.

One octopus has a strange way of hunting. The blanket octopus gets its name from the long, shiny cape around its arms. The cape makes the octopus look bigger.

But the blanket octopus also has a secret weapon . . . it is not hurt by jellyfish stings. *Grab!* It yanks off a jellyfish tentacle and is not harmed. *Stab!* It uses the jellyfish tentacle to kill a fish.

Only the female blanket octopus can do this. She is about six feet long, but the male is only one *inch* long. This size difference between female and male is the biggest of any animal in the world!

Almost all octopuses hunt at night to avoid danger. The day octopus hunts mostly during the daytime. It has to be extra sneaky to not be seen.

The day octopus changes shape to be fat, skinny, or tall. It is also called the big blue octopus because it can have blue spots on its body. It can even create

bumps all over its skin to make itself look like a piece of coral.

This octopus is strong and fierce. *Zip!* It pulls a crab off a rock. *Rip!* It tears the crab apart. It will even eat a smaller octopus of its own kind.

Thinking Fast

Octopuses have to make
a lot of choices about how
to hide and hunt. They have
one brain in their head and
a mini-brain in each arm. An
octopus has nine separate but
connected brains!

Scientists have studied
the common octopus a lot.
It is a very curious creature.
Sometimes it plays with objects
such as jars to see what is
inside. Some scientists believe
this play means that octopuses
are as smart as dolphins and
dogs. Wow!

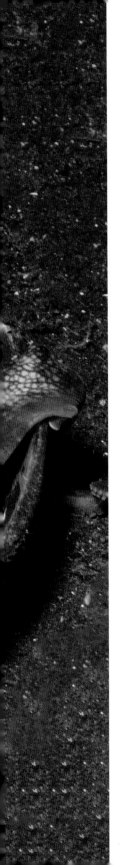

Using tools is one important way that animals show they are smart. The veined octopus is famous for using a strange object as its home. It rests in coconut shells!

There are lots of empty coconut shells in the water where the veined octopus lives. *Flop!* It turns over a shell and climbs in. The octopus hangs its arms out. It walks like a spider while moving the shell. *Plop!* It collects both parts of a shell and closes them up. What a clever octopus!

Many octopuses that live in aquariums have shown how smart they are. Some octopuses have learned how to open locks and turn off light switches.

Other octopuses have taken off the lids to their tanks and escaped. They crawl across the floor and into other aquarium tanks. They eat the creatures inside and then return home.

Squeeze! Octopuses can get into tiny spaces because they do not have bones. One octopus even escaped through a floor drain. It slid down a pipe and returned to the ocean!

Another way that octopuses show their smarts is by their personalities. Some octopuses are shy while others are daring. Some are lazy and others are more playful.

Octopuses show these personalities when they interact with people. They like some people better than others. They touch people with their arms to get to know them. *Splash!* An annoyed octopus will squirt a person with water. Silly octopus!

Are octopuses the smartest swimmers in the sea? We do not know for sure yet. But one thing is certain. Octopuses are fascinating, fast-thinking creatures!